BARNABY'S FRIENDS
AND FANS HAVE SPOKEN...

"A SERIES OF COMIC STRIPS WHICH, LAID END TO END, REACH FROM HERE TO WHEREVER YOU WANT TO GO JUST ONCE BEFORE YOU DIE."
—*The New York Times*

"I WANT TO RECOMMEND *BARNABY* FOR THE CHRISTMAS STOCKINGS OF ALL PARENTS, UNCLES, AND OTHER ADULTS IN GOOD STANDING." —*Chicago Sunday Tribune*

"THE GREATEST BOOK SINCE *WAR AND PEACE*." —J.J. O'Malley

"CROCKETT JOHNSON'S *BARNABY* COMES AS A BREATH OF SWEET, COOL AIR."
—*Life Magazine*

BARNABY BOOKS
Published by Ballantine Books

#1 WANTED: A FAIRY GODFATHER
#2 MR. O'MALLEY AND THE HAUNTED HOUSE
#3 JACKEEN J. O'MALLEY FOR CONGRESS
#4 MR. O'MALLEY GOES FOR THE GOLD
#5 MR. O'MALLEY, WIZARD OF WALL STREET*
#6 J.J. O'MALLEY GOES HOLLYWOOD*

—AND LOTS MORE TO COME...

*Forthcoming

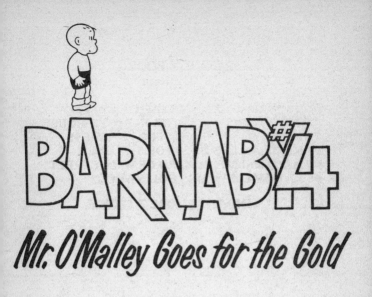

BARNABY #4

Mr. O'Malley Goes for the Gold

by

CROCKETT JOHNSON

A Del Rey Book
Ballantine Books • New York

A Mash Note From A Great Lady...
Dorothy Parker

(This letter appeared in PM October 3, 1943 upon release of the first hardcover published by Henry Holt & Co.)

I cannot write a review of Crockett Johnson's book of Barnaby. I have tried and tried, but it never comes out a book review. It is always a valentine for Mr. Johnson.

For a bulky segment of a century, I have been an avid follower of comic strips—all comic strips; this is a statement made with approximately the same amount of pride with which one would say, "I've been shooting cocaine into my arm for the past 25 years." I cannot remember how the habit started, and I am certainly unable to explain why it persists. I know only that I'm hooked, by now, that's all. I can't stop. I even take a certain unspeakable tabloid for its strips, though, when I am caught with it on my doorstep, I still have shame enough left to try to laugh matters off by explaining that you really ought to know what your enemies are up to. When I will tell you that I am in daily touch with the horrible, sightless, Orphan Annie—who, I am convinced, is Westbrook Pegler's adopted child—that I keep up with the particular nasty experiences of Dick Tracy, that even, for heaven's sake, I was the one who strung along with Deathless Deer until her mercy killing, you will know that Mother is a gone pigeon. When cornered, I try to make rather doggy excuses. I say that comic strips are important pieces of Americana. But it doesn't hold, you know. You cannot class the relationship between Flash Gordon and Dale as something peculiarly American. I flatly do not know why I do as I do. For I do not enjoy the strips. I read them solemnly and sourly, and there is no delight in me because of them.

That is, I had no delight and no enjoyment and no love until Barnaby came. I suppose you must do it this way; I suppose you must file Barnaby under comic strips, because his biography runs along in strip form in a newspaper. I bow to convention in the matter. But, privately, if the adventures of Barnaby constitute a comic strip, then so do those of Huckleberry Finn.

I think, and I am trying to talk calmly, that Barnaby and his friends and oppressors are the most important additions to

American arts and letters in Lord knows how many years. I know that they are the most important additions to my heart. I love Barnaby, I love little Jane, I love Gus, the Ghost, I hate and admire and envy Mr. O'Malley, above all I love Gorgon, the dog.

I think the conception of a dog who talks—"Didn't know I could do it; never tried it before, I guess"—and then turns out to be such a crashing bore that they have to lock him away so they won't be obliged to listen to him, is—well, it's only glorious, that's all. You have to love dogs before you can go on to the step of taking them down, understandingly. I think Mr. Johnson must love dogs. I think Mr. Johnson must love people. I know darned well I must love Mr. Johnson.

Barnaby is fine to have in book form—you can't go on, you know, cutting strips out of PM and meaning to paste them in an album the next rainy day. The book will be invaluable to those who must read aloud a while every evening. I am told, by those fortunates who own them, that children love Barnaby; which information has appreciably raised my estimate of children. While for adults—I can only say *Barnaby*, the book, costs $2. If you have $5, save out three for the landlord and spend the remainder to feed your soul.

Well. I told you I couldn't write anything but a valentine, didn't I?

—DOROTHY PARKER

1

2

CROCKETT JOHNSON

5

But Mom said nobody can go.in Pop's room, Mr. O'Malley, while the doctor's there . . .

I'm not allowed? Me? Your Good Fairy Godfather? Not permitted to perform an errand of mercy? To succor your stricken father? To comfort? To heal? To listen in on the Doc's stethoscope? . . .

My pipe's out again, O'Malley.

CROCKETT JOHNSON

How patiently I've waited for calamity to strike this home . . . NOW, when I'm needed MOST—Gridley, have you EVER, in your long career as a Salamander—

I got to get back to the firehouse . . .

But—

I'll go along with you. I'm not wanted here . . . Sorry, Gridley, I haven't any more matches . . . But, say! I'll be glad to teach you how to rub two sticks together—

Copyright 1944 Field Publications

8

9

Panel 1:
Easy, isn't it, Gridley? ... Just rub the two sticks together ... It takes a bit of time. Rome wasn't burnt in a day, you know ... As Nero so neatly—

Barnaby! Hello!

5-18

Panel 2:
-I was thinking of you, m'boy ... Of how, unintentionally, I may have been a bit curt to you ... Of how much you'll enjoy the outdoor barbecue I'm planning, when Gridley starts that fire ...

Panel 3:
... Of how you'll enjoy my tales of the days of "Dan" Boone and "Dan" Beard and "Dan" O'Malley, as they called me, when we sit huddled around the dying embers after we've all eaten our full ...

What are we going to eat? ...

Panel 4:
CROCKETT JOHNSON

Copyright 1942 Field Publications

I was also thinking, m'boy, of what we might find in the way of comestibles in—er—your pantry.

Mr. O'Malley. You can help Pop—

Your father! . . . Has his malady taken a turn for the worse? Cushlamochree! . . .

5-19

The Doc has given up in despair? A hopeless case! . . . I'll pull him through! . . . Run ahead, Barnaby. Sterilize the forceps! . . . Aspirin! Have a lot of pans full of boiling water . . . And Vitamin B tablets . . .

No. Pop's cold is better—

CROCKETT JOHNSON

I'll need an old kitchen table! . . . And an oxygen tent . . . Open a can of plasma . . . Get some good books on faith healing . . . And all the sulfa drugs! . . . Leeches—

But—

I'll bring the serum myself! I'll round up a team of huskies—

Copyright 1944 Field Publications

11

I've completed a tour of inspection of the atelier your father works in. An Efficiency Expert is just what that plant needs!...

Gosh, are you one?

5·23

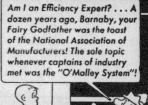

Am I an Efficiency Expert?... A dozen years ago, Barnaby, your Fairy Godfather was the toast of the National Association of Manufacturers! The sole topic whenever captains of industry met was the "O'Malley System"!

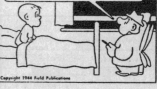

Industrialists rushed to their mills to argue my theories with the watchman... Business men, discussing my efficiency plan on street corners, neglected their little pyramids of apples...

CROCKETT JOHNSON

So eagerly did management study the O'Malley System of Ausgestretchupgespeed, as it was known internationally, that very little work was done. In fact, NO work was done...

Gosh.

14

John . . . The doctor said to stay in bed.

I want to call the plant . . .

5·25

Mitchell? John Baxter . . . How are things going? . . . Where's the production curve— It's gone up? . . . Great! . . . By the way, who's taking care of the chart while I'm away? . . .

TOTAL PRODUCTION

I don't know, John. . . . I think Burns is doing it. Or Mac—

Copyright 1944 Field Publications

CROCKETT JOHNSON

Yes. Production shows a slight rise . . . Can't expect too much, Barnaby . . . It's my first day on the job.

I'm much better, thanks. I'll be back at work in a couple of days . . . Does the chart still show production is up? Fine! . . .

5-27

They'll hand out the Army-Navy "E" for that production record—

The Army-Navy "E" . . . I'll tell Mr. O'Malley . . .

My Fairy Godfather will be glad to hear the Army and Navy will appreciate all the work he's doing . . .

Copyright 1944 Field Publications

CROCKETT JOHNSON

Mr. O'Malley!

ARMY

NAVY

E

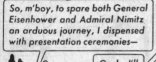
So, m'boy, to spare both General Eisenhower and Admiral Nimitz an arduous journey, I dispensed with presentation ceremonies—

Gosh. I'll tell Pop—

5-29 Copyright 1944 Field Publications

Mom, Mr. O'Malley, my Fairy Godfather, got the Army-Navy "E"...

Oh, hush, Barnaby—

I'm going downtown to shop. Don't disturb your father...

But, Mom—

& VEGETABLES

CROCKETT JOHNSON

19

CROCKETT JOHNSON

Copyright 1946 Field Publications

21

Panel 1:
Mom. Mr. O'Malley, my Fairy Godfather, fixed things so Pop won't think the factory can get on better without him...

6-5 Copyright 1946 Field Publications

Panel 2:
Production was going down. And ever since Pop got sick it's been going up. But when Pop phones the office today—

He's not going to call the office...

CROCKETT JOHNSON

Panel 3:
Your father's going back to work this morning, Barnaby.

HUH?

Panel 4:
Take it easy today, John... And don't let anything upset you...

But— Gosh!

A Pixey this size! How could any work he's able to do make the production graph of that big factory go up and down?

Mr. O'Malley's very amazing—

Glad you're back, John—Can't stop! Awful mess! The boss is wild! The plant's in a panic!—

But what's the matter? With the production record you've all been setting, I expected—

Look, John—

EXECUTIVE OFFICE

Copyright 1944 Field Publications

TOTAL PRODUCTION

CROCKETT JOHNSON

I'll be home soon, Ellen... We've checked the output of all the departments... Production's been going along on an even keel!

6-7

It was only that big display graph that caused a panic. Its ups and downs show no relation to actual figures.

But, who did it?...

Everyone here says he thought someone else had been taking care of it while I was away... Well WHOEVER did it must be somebody out of this world—

CROCKETT JOHNSON

Pop's working late, Mr. O'Malley—

No trouble, I hope. I'll be glad to run down to the office and help out again.

27

Panel 1:
Of course your father found no correlation between that graph and production figures. ... I hadn't got around yet to fitting the data to the curve.

Oh.

Panel 2:
Everyone seemed agreed that the production curve was the important thing. Naturally, I do important things FIRST—

There's Jane—

CROCKETT
JOHNSON

Panel 3:
Your dad isn't up on modern statistical methods, m'boy—

Barnaby. I saw a dopey little man near the woods—

Panel 4:
With a fireman's hat. And he's rubbing two sticks together—

Gridley, the Fire Pixey! I forgot all about him—

29

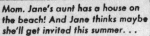

Mom. Jane's aunt has a house on the beach! And Jane thinks maybe she'll get invited this summer...

How nice.

And Mr. O'Malley, my Fairy Godfather, says that maybe Jane might invite me...

Well, don't make any plans on all those "maybe's", Barnaby—

Oh, no, Mom. I wasn't making PLANS. I just mentioned it...

CROCKETT JOHNSON

PADDY'S SIDEWALK CAFÉ

Mr. O'Malley!

...But gosh, Mr. O'Malley... If Jane hasn't been invited to her aunt's cottage at the beach, Jane can't invite ME—

6-12   Copyright 1944 Field Publications

That aunt!...The thoughtlessness of the woman! Allowing a mere formality to defeat your Fairy Godfather's effort to give you a beneficial vacation at the shore! Away from the hot city streets—

Hot city streets?

The realtor who sold your dad his property out here ADMITTED the development is becoming a teeming metropolis, a modern Babylon—But let's not quibble...

I'm certain after I present the complete heart-rending story to Jane's aunt, she'll—

You're going to SEE her?

CROCKETT JOHNSON

31

CROCKETT JOHNSON

Copyright 1946 Field Publications

This is a grand place.

It's perfect! Away from everything...

No one around... Not even Barnaby's imaginary Pixey—

Where is he?...

Hey, Barnaby! There's your Fairy Godfather! Look! He's out fishing!

Where, Jane?

CROCKETT JOHNSON

Copyright 1944 Field Publications

Oh, no. It's only a gull...

41

But Mr. O'Malley, my Fairy Godfather, said he'd be here! What ever happened to him?

Let's build a sand fort.

G 24

Sure is quiet here. You'd never think there's one of those hectic amusement parks a mile up the beach, would you, John? With a breakneck roller coaster and a—

Huh?

Copyright 1944 Field Publications

A breakneck roller coaster! Gee, Barnaby, I don't blame you for being worried about your Fairy Godfather! Gee!

CROCKETT JOHNSON

Well... As long as I know where he IS—

Let's build a sand fort, Jane.

I invited Gus out here, m'boy. Sun and fresh air will help get rid of that pallor of his.

Where are you staying?

I realized this cottage was a bit crowded, and, also, for my gregarious taste, a bit remote. So I engaged quarters in the amusement park down there—

In a hotel?

No. Normally our landlord doesn't take lodgers... But it's a fine place, Gus, isn't it? ... Running water and—

Copyright 1944 Field Publications

CROCKETT JOHNSON

It's a papier mâché grotto in the "Tunnel of Horrors"!

Gosh!

Our grotto in the "Tunnel of Horrors" makes an ideal lodging... Right in the center of the gay amusement area. Handy to the roller coaster and a frozen custard kiosk... Those tableaus in the other niches won't startle you, Gus, when you get used to them... They're only waxworks—

It isn't that, O'Malley...

Is Gus scared, Mr. O'Malley?

6-30 Copyright 1944 Field Publications

It's those boatloads of Fiends that float by in the dark! At regular intervals! Screeching—

Rain's stopped. We should be getting back...

CROCKETT JOHNSON

Last boat goes through at two o'clock... Come see us, m'boy. Give these to the man outside.

Gosh. Two tickets...

47

The pirates wouldn't hide their treasure down near the cottage colony. Nor up by the amusement area... Too many nosey people.

7-9

That leaves only two miles of beach for us to dig up... See, m'boy, how my scientific brain narrows the problem?...

Two miles?

Copyright 1946 Field Publications

Still quite a chore, isn't it? And that recent storm has obliterated any eighteenth century footprints or other clues they may have left— But, say! If we had a MAP!

There's a big book of maps in our cottage, Mr. O'Malley, but—

Excellent! Come, Barnaby! Let's not waste any time...

CROCKETT JOHNSON

50

How's that for a pirate treasure map? Note the skull and cross bones...

Well...

But—

7-5

Yes. I'm a skilled cartographer. ...I mapped out a route to the headwaters of the Nile. For Dr. Livingstone... Dr. Cook set off to the Pole with my maps...

Big jobs... Small ones... I originally determined the boundaries of Peru, Bolivia, and Colombia... I laid out a couple of adjacent tracts of land for two bosom friends named Hatfield and McCoy.

But, now, let's find that gold... This map shows an old oak tree. And—

But there are no oak trees—

CROCKETT JOHNSON

51

55

CROCKETT
JOHNSON

An old friend of Mr. O'Malley gave them to me. Mr. Jones. . . . He's King of the Sea and he's got a pitchfork. . . And—

It's no use. . .

7-15 Copyright 1944 Field Publications

That big storm must have churned up the beach and Barnaby found those Pieces of Eight somewhere—

But if we knew where—

Pop. . . Mr. O'Malley, my Fairy Godfather, knows where the treasure is. He made a pirate map—

Never mind. . . We'll take pot luck. . . Digging along 'side of everybody else. . .

CROCKETT JOHNSON

60

I've decided against employing that big salvage corporation... I phoned, asking them to rush a vessel and diving crew out here for that pirate treasure. They showed quite an interest.

7-18 Copyright 1944 Field Publications

Especially when I told them all about myself. And about my old pirate map, which I—

You made the map yourself—

Yes. I stressed that point. To show I personally could vouch for its accuracy... The girl at the switchboard was impressed, but when her boy friend called up on another wire, she said she'd have to call me back...

CROCKETT JOHNSON

I gave her the number of the skee ball establishment and I told her to have me paged in "The Tunnel of Horrors"... But she never called... Awfully lax way of doing business, isn't it?

Mustering a crew for our treasure cruise isn't any problem. ·. You. And Gus, when he's fully recovered—

Gus, the Ghost? He's been sick?

7-20 Copyright 1944 Field Publications

Yes. I persuaded Gus to try to get brown as a berry. . . I didn't realize how unused to sun baths Ghosts are. Their work, you know, keeps them—

Is Gus sunburned?

Merely a second-degree burn. He'll be well again and eager to ship out in a day or so—

And you'll have a boat by then, Mr. O'Malley?

CROCKETT JOHNSON

How will you get the boat? . . . By waving your magic cigar?

I may do that. . . Or wire Henry Kaiser. . . Or, mmm, let me see.

70

I can tell you what we'll find, Barnaby. We'll find your boat floating off shore because the string has been taken off it. There won't be any Pixies near it—

The Leprechaun is sailing it—

Mr. O'Malley, my Fairy Godfather, is there. Trying to get it back—

7-31

See. No Leprechaun nor anything else is sailing that boat. And—

Mr. O'Malley isn't here!

Gee. How did your father know your Fairy Godfather wouldn't be here? . . .

It's amazing, Jane. . . . Maybe he knows when Mr. O'Malley will get back, too.

CROCKETT JOHNSON

73

O'Malley's not even going to try to get back this year...

He's too smart...

Mr. O'Malley, my Fairy Godfather, has to come back here! To get the pirate treasure!

This can't interest you, Barnaby. We're talking about the election and Congressman O'Malley. Not that imaginary Pixey of yours. Run along—

O'Malley's friends keep an ear to the ground...

Yes, George. I'm sure O'Malley's close political advisors know exactly what they're doing—

Barnaby! What are you doing?

I don't know, Pop. Mr. Shultz said—

CROCKETT JOHNSON

75

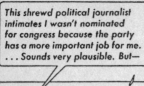

This shrewd political journalist intimates I wasn't nominated for congress because the party has a more important job for me. . . . Sounds very plausible. But—

8-5

Ah! Yes! They need the wise counsel we elder statesmen can bring to the campaign's problems. . . Like Mr. Hoover. But before I begin, m'boy, we must find that pirate gold. . .

Copyright 1944 Field Publications

A sizable campaign contribution will not be amiss. Now that I'm making all strategic decisions—

Will you give all that gold to the party?

CROCKETT JOHNSON

To the OTHER party. . . To even things up, sportingly.

Also to hedge a bit on a little ambassadorship I've had my eye on. . .

But, Mr. Jones said he can't help us with the treasure.

I won't ask him to help us FIND it, Barnaby. I don't want him to break any of the rules... All we want from Davy is an estimate of the value of its contents...

He'll tell us that much, surely. When he gets in an expansive mood. After we've wined and dined him in a lavish manner—

Are you taking him to dinner? Where?

Oh, any establishment where the cuisine meets my exacting requirements—Ah! I have it!

YOUR COTTAGE... Your mother won't mind setting a couple of extra places...

CROCKETT JOHNSON

CROCKETT JOHNSON

Mr. O'Malley, my Fairy Godfather, will be here soon, I hope, and—

Don't you like that book, Gus?

Gracious! Oh! My goodness! Eeeek!

8-19

Oh, yes. It's fascinating, but— Listen! Do you hear footsteps? Stealthy ones! Sinister and—

You're imagining things, Gus...

Copyright 1944 Field Publications

Perhaps I am... The dangerous mission O'Malley has planned for us. And this book—LOOK! The window! A hideous face!

Huh?

Well, how are you intrepid adventurers tonight, eh?

Gus! Come out... It's Mr. O'Malley.

CROCKETT JOHNSON

Sorry I'm late, m'boy. I had a bit of trouble getting the equipment together for our treasure cruise. This sea-sickness remedy—Gus!

Gus was reading this book. And—

Amazing how widespread interest in the supernatural is becoming. The stress of the times, I suppose. A pathetic attempt to flee from a turbulent world's real problems...

Hmmm...

Mr. O'Malley. If we're going to find that treasure—

Eh? Oh, yes... I'll be right there... Say, Barnaby... If nobody's reading this, can I borrow it tomorrow?...

Copyright 1944 Field Publications

91

You can't upset all my carefully laid plans, Gus! Besides, there's no danger in undersea work... Not with this new and improved diving bell of mine... Look...

No!... No, O'Malley!

It looks just like a pail...

Yes, Barnaby, it does resemble a pail somewhat, doesn't it? Except that its aperture is at the bottom... The air is held in a diving bell by the pressure of the water from below, you see. And—

Did you invent it?

Copyright 1946 Field Publications

No. I merely improved it. The air in the conventional bell tends to become stuffy. And vision is bad. So I punched these holes in it...

Slip it on, Gus. For size—

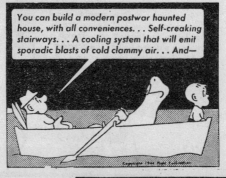

Shouldn't we have turned that boxful of maps in for waste paper, Mr. O'Malley?

They were parchment. Besides, I have solved the paper shortage...

The Newspaper Publishers Association will be delighted by my simple plan. It merely calls for the elimination of comic strips.

Will that save enough—GOSH!

Glub!

M'boy, statistics show that 96 percent of readers peruse the comics. And will it be worthwhile to print the remainder of the newspaper for the other 4 percent? ... No ... So, the presses can be sold for scrap—you see, I think of everything—

Mr. O'Malley! We forgot all about Gus! ...

CROCKETT JOHNSON

John! Barnaby's not in his bed! . . . John! Wake up!

9-1

He did say something about hunting a treasure. With his imaginary Fairy Godfather and a Ghost he calls "Gus".

The trouble that kid's dream creatures cause! Isn't there SOME way to get rid of them—

There he is!

Mom! Pop! Gus, the Ghost, got DROWNED!

CROCKETT JOHNSON

I'm in a quandary, m'boy. . . . Trying to learn what's happened to poor Gus—

He jumped into the water and didn't come up—

I know that, Barnaby. But why DIDN'T he? . . . All the authorities on folklore I've consulted agree that Ghosts are indestructible. . .

So Gus might be all right?

Possibly. But Ghosts are made of ectoplasm, you know. . . I looked up the chemical ingredients of ectoplasm. In "Henley's Formulas for Home, Farm and Workshop."

CROCKETT JOHNSON

And they're all soluble in water!

Gosh! Poor Gus!

No, Barnaby... No news of Gus yet. I've about given up hope.

Maybe Gus the Ghost is at his haunted house.

9-7

Gus is considerate enough to have notified us in that case. To spare me all this heartache and worry... But I may stroll down to his residence at that.

CROCKETT JOHNSON

The least I can do for poor Gus is to take care of his personal belongings. Put his papers in order. And—

Say!

I just remembered!... A few years ago a very determined underwriter sold my friend Gus an INSURANCE POLICY!

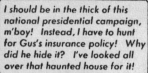
I should be in the thick of this national presidential campaign, m'boy! Instead, I have to hunt for Gus's insurance policy! Why did he hide it? I've looked all over that haunted house for it!

. . . Election is less than two months away and I haven't even engaged my national campaign quarters yet! . . .

I have to spend my valuable time searching that old house—

Cushlamochree! That old house!

Come along, Barnaby. . . See if you don't think Gus's old mansion is just the place for my election headquarters!

CROCKETT JOHNSON

Copyright 1944 Field Publications

CROCKETT JOHNSON

Yes, m'boy. My behind-the-scenes national headquarters will carry a heavy load this campaign . . .

Copyright 1944 Field Publications

Here I'll hold many weighty discussions of our platform with very big people! Great statesmen, titans of commerce, mammoth industrialists, giant financiers! Getting their reactions as we run over each plank—

CROCKETT JOHNSON

About time you got to this conference. My name's Wurst. This is Ex-Senator Ecks... Which of you is J. J. O'Malley?

He is... He's my Fairy Godfather.

9 29

Barnaby! It's Colonel Wurst! The patriotic publisher who prints his American editions of the *Voelkischer Beobachter* in red white and blue ink...

J.J., this is A.A.

Copyright 1944 Field Publications

I brought A.A. along to give us the direct, uncolored views of a 'Man in the Street'...

Sell short, young fellow, sell short.

Huh?

CROCKETT JOHNSON

126

127

Jane says Barnaby's at that deserted house playing with those Pixies and Ghosts he dreams up... You'll have to look for him, John. It's dark—

10-7

It's time to begin worrying if that kid's so engrossed in imaginary creatures he doesn't realize when it's way past his suppertime—

Here he is!

CROCKETT JOHNSON

Hello. Is lunch ready?

But the Tycoon's watch said it was noon, Mom. And Mr. O'Malley, my Fairy Godfather, read it was noon in Colonel Wurst's newspaper. So—

He's plagiarizing Lewis Carroll, Ellen. The Mad Hatter's endless tea party. The clock stopped at—

CROCKETT JOHNSON

No. This is very different, Pop. . . The Tycoon's watch runs. But backwards. So—

Backwards? But, why—

Copyright 1944 Field Publications

Pop. Will I like it back in the good old days?

See...Mr. O'Malley and the Ghosts ARE having that political meeting here in the haunted house. In a smoke-filled room...

I was right, wasn't I, Pop?—Aren't you coming inside? And meet—

I'll run down to Hanson's Dairy! To phone in an alarm! The house is on FIRE! Wait right here, son—

It's on FIRE?... Gosh!...I had better rescue Mr. O'Malley!

CROCKETT JOHNSON

CROCKETT JOHNSON

No sign of a fire here. I smell tobacco smoke. Somebody with a cigar, probably. Just looking around the empty old house—

But smoke POURED out that window!

Next time, mister, investigate before you phone... Know what false alarms cost each year? And most of them come in from nuts who like to see fire engines—

Listen! ... I'm no nut! I'm a sober citizen who—er —happened to stroll by. And—

CROCKETT JOHNSON

Why did your old man turn in the alarm, kid?

He came up here to see if my Fairy Godfather and three Ghosts were having a meeting. And—

BARNABY!

Copyright 1944 Field Publications

143

CROCKETT JOHNSON

Copyright 1944 Field Publications

148

No extraneous matters must influence the election, gentlemen. If the war's doing that, there's only one fair thing to do, isn't there? Call off the war!

I've said that in my editorials, too. But I'm afraid it's too late—

Too late, Colonel Wurst?... It's only 1938 by my watch.

CROCKETT JOHNSON

Copyright 1944 Field Publications

You're right, A.A., as usual . . . A cable just arrived from Munich.

But—

PEACE IN OUR TIME

No, Barnaby. Our meeting's not over. I stepped out for a day or so. The Ex-Senator is concluding a filibuster over our platform plank dealing with Education . . .

Publisher Wurst is strong for Education. Up to the third grade . . . But the Ex-Senator steadfastly is opposing this.

He wants all schools abolished. Claims they're subversive . . . An investigation he headed found they teach people how to write.

Copyright 1944 Field Publications

You see, he was defeated in the primaries by a write-in vote . . .

CROCKETT JOHNSON

156

Copyright 1944 Field Publications

CROCKETT JOHNSON

161

There aren't any turkeys in these woods... Besides the government says we all have to eat something else this Thanksgiving—

Barnaby, this case is different. Myles needs a Turkey to set a precedent. He's got to take it up to Plymouth. For the FIRST Thanksgiving. It's important—

11-15

CROCKETT JOHNSON

But how can it be the FIRST Thanksgiving. We had one last year. And the year before—

Myles has been hunting a turkey for sometime—

...For years?

Yes, m'boy. For years... But your quest is just about over, Myles... You'll get a turkey.

Let me have that musket.

Here's a nutty news item, Ellen. The cops picked up a hunter in a red hat who ran out of the woods claiming a pheasant he'd fired at SHOT BACK at him! ...

They kept him at the station house to sober up. But he still insists that, just as he pulled the trigger on a big bird, which had flown up over the bushes—

How silly.

CROCKETT JOHNSON

11-16 Copyright 1944 Field Publications

So, m'boy, I flew up over the bushes and pointed Myles' musket right at the bird. I knew it was a turkey by a glimpse of red comb on his head.

And, exactly as I pulled the trigger, the turkey fired right back at ME! ... It was—unbelievable!

Verily!

The reason most people fail to win raffles, Barnaby, is because they don't buy the lucky ticket—

But you did?

11-21

I selected my ticket with great care... And here I am with the turkey! I just got him out of the crate in the backyard of Paddy's Bar and Grill ... I shrewdly chose number 76,392,864,753-B!

And it WON!

It hasn't won yet, officially. You see, the drawing won't be held until TOMORROW.

Oh.

CROCKETT JOHNSON

170

177

This is kind of a slow way to get Mom a Christmas present, isn't it? Sitting here waiting for a trapper to bring in an ermine. And how about Pop—

His gift is easy . . . A carton of cigarettes.

FUR TRADING POST
John Jacob O'Malley
PROP

FLOUR

12-5

In fact I'm taking care of that right this very minute. Working very hard on it—

But you're just sitting there—

CROCKETT JOHNSON

Hush, Barnaby. Before I can get your dad that carton of cigarettes, I've got to solve the problem of the nation's tobacco shortage. Let's see—

FUR TR
n Ja

184

I've hunted lions, and dragons, bears, multi-headed serpentine monsters, and squirrels . . . But I've never run across the animals you describe, O'Malley

Neither have I.

Wily beasts, aren't they? Keeping out of sight like that . . . Well, let me see—

I have it! . . . Orion, old pal, we'll lure an ermine out of hiding! . . . With a DECOY! . . . We'll build a likeness of one of the huge white beasts. Out of SNOW! . . . Snow is often imagined to be an ermine mantle, isn't it? So—

But—Is it going to snow?

CROCKETT JOHNSON

Yes. I think I definitely can predict it. It snows every winter, doesn't it—

That's true—

187

197

It's the only way it could have happened, Officer. The thieves' car crashed. So they carried the furs off and hid them. But they dropped the ermine wrap somewhere. And Barnaby found it and he brought it home.

And the kid made up the O'Malley guy in his head?

Yes. He's a very imaginative child. And—

But Mr. O'Malley said Orion got an ermine skin after all. He found it in the morning in the shed. So Orion must have left it there for him—

O'RYAN?

CROCKETT JOHNSON

Copyright 1946 Field Publications

Now don't tell me the kid made up this O'Ryan, too! We KNOW this is one of Sables O'Ryan's jobs. See?

Operator? I want a policeman— I mean—Get me Headquarters!

But—

202

CROCKETT JOHNSON

Copyright 1944 Field Publications

Your old Fairy Godfather will find a way to absolve your dad, Barnaby. Mmm. But he's in quite a jam . . . Cops in the house. . . . Those stolen furs in his cellar—

You put the furs there—

CROCKETT JOHNSON

Warn him to say nothing. Until I bring a battery of competent counselors, who, under my direction, will—

But, no! I can't do that.

Every GOOD lawyer limits his lucrative practice exclusively to the defense of comely young women, or their honest fiancés, falsely accused, by dull-witted district attorneys, of MURDER—

I've read all the cases on the shelf in the drugstore, and—

Mr. O'Malley! The policemen! They're coming upstairs! . . .

Of course. Search the house. I insist on it!

We'll start in the attic.

I'd better tell the cops the furs are down in the cellar.

I doubt if that will allay their suspicion, m'boy.

I've read many parallel cases. The only way falsely suspected people prove their innocence is by apprehending the really guilty perpetrators themselves.

We must forestall the police. Until I've brought the case to a brilliant conclusion . . .

I must act quickly!

CROCKETT JOHNSON

CROCKETT
JOHNSON

Copyright 1945 Field Publications

209

If you had those Gnomes take the furs out of our cellar, Mr. O'Malley, the police won't bother Pop anymore. But where did the Gnomes put the furs?

I—er—don't know exactly. But the important thing is that now I can begin to solve the original robbery. Unhampered by dull and unimaginative policemen—

1-6

When I've apprehended and secured the culprits, I'll turn them over to the authorities. In the quiet, modest, self-effacing manner we celebrated independent investigators adhere to—

But—

The police, the proprietor of the fur store, the insurance people, my publisher, will be very happy—

But if you don't know where the furs are . . .

CROCKETT JOHNSON

Copyright 1945 Field Publications

210

The cops didn't find them hot furs we stashed in that shed when the car smashed up. So what ever happened to them?

How did they get the ermine wrap?

That fellow Baxter claims his kid found it . . . Say, I wonder about that guy . . .

But, Sables, if he convinced the cops—

Maybe we're a little bit smarter than the cops. See if Baxter's in the phone book.

The police are satisfied now that Barnaby found the fur wrap outdoors. So we won't hear anymore about THAT—

There's the telephone—

CROCKETT JOHNSON

Copyright 1943 Field Publication

No. I've no word yet from the fur thieves, Lieutenant. Oh, by the way. The private detective the fur company hired was here last night.

I outlined our plan to trap the gang—What? No, I didn't ask to see his badge. Or papers—

I saw his badge, Pop . . . Jane has one just like it. She got it from Whoopie Flakes. For two boxtops—

Nonsense, Barnaby—

Copyright 1945 Field Publications

CROCKETT JOHNSON

The fur company has nobody ON the case!

Then, who—Goodness!

215

ABOUT THE AUTHOR

Born in New York of Scottish parents, Crockett Johnson's only formal art training was a six-months' stint at Cooper Union, drawing from plaster casts and studying typography. His first job was with Macy's advertising department, from which he resigned—just before he was fired for wearing a soft collar instead of the regulation stiff one.

Before settling down to work on *Barnaby* in 1942, Johnson was art director for McGraw-Hill and a free-lance cartoonist whose most popular feature, "The Little Man with the Eyes," appeared regularly in *Collier's*. His children's book—*Harold and the Purple Crayon*—is one of the great classics.

BARNABY IS BACK!

Laugh along with Johnson Crockett's delightful characters: Jackeen J. O'Malley, the Fairy Godfather whose magic wand is a cigar; Gus the Ghost; McSnoyd the Invisible Leprechaun, and a host of others in this whimsical, magical collection. "*Barnaby* was one of the great comic strips of all time." —Charles M. Shulz